ADVENTURES OF GRAMMY AND ME
GOING ON A HIKE

ELLEN LODICO

Outskirts Press, Inc.
http://www.outskirtspress.com

ISBN: 978-1-9772-1610-6

Illustrated by Richa Kinra
Illustrations © 2021 Outskirts Press, Inc. All rights reserved - used with permission.

Outskirts Press and the "OP" logo are trademarks belonging to Outskirts Press, Inc.

PRINTED IN THE UNITED STATES OF AMERICA

I would like to dedicate this book to my beautiful daughter Jennifer.

She has taught me, a city born woman, to see the beauty in nature and all animals, big and small. May she always find peace in the natural beauty that surrounds us and keeps moving it forward!

This Book Belongs to:

_____

It's that time again! Summertime! School is about to be over for my summer break and I will be visiting my Grammy. It's the best time for me. I visit her every summer. We have so much fun together when I visit!

When I spoke to Grammy, she said "I have some new, fun ideas we can try this summer." We always find fun things to do! Grammy is always trying to get me to do new things. Sometimes, I don't like to try new things. I like to stick with the same things that I'm used to, but I am learning it's okay to try because most of the time it turns out to be really great!

Mom helped me pack a suitcase, and as soon as school was over, I was ready to go!

This year when I got to Grammy's house, she was very excited to see me. She wanted to show me some special clothes she bought for me. They were hanging in my room.

I saw long pants, long sleeve shirt and a new hat. I asked Grammy "Why do I have these strange looking clothes?"

The clothing was a dark green color, which I did not think was pretty and bright. Grammy answered, "They are hiking clothes."

The clothes are meant to protect me from bugs and good for walking in the woods.

"Why do I need special clothes?" I asked. I like bugs, and they are so small, I did not think I needed protection from bugs.

Grammy explained that we were going to go on some nature hikes this summer. There are many ticks and mosquitos in the woods that can bite your skin. Bug bites can itch, and make us feel uncomfortable. These clothes will protect us from those biting bugs.

Then, Grammy ran into her room and came back with the same clothes, just bigger! "Look, I have the same outfit!", she said.

Oh boy! Grammy is going to take me on another adventure!

After a few days at Grammy's, she said it's a beautiful day today let's go on our first nature hike!

Grammy brought out our new clothes and we put them on. They felt lightweight and the pants had a lot of pockets. My favorite was the hat. She said that it would protect my head and my hair. I just love hats. They're fun to wear!

Grammy drove us to a nearby lake. She said this would be a good place to start. It had some grassy areas and a lot of trees around.

I saw people in sail boats on the lake. Some people were in their canoes and were fishing. It looked pretty. We saw some squirrels jumping from one tree to another and people walking dogs.

We continued walking and enjoying the sights. Then, Grammy saw a small bridge that allowed us to walk to the other side of the lake. "Let's take the bridge", Grammy said, "and see what's on the other side."

We stopped on the bridge and looked into the water. I saw some fish swimming around. Then Grammy saw some turtles, and asked me to count them. I counted nine of them. It was so much fun to see how many I could find.

Then we saw two big swans and a bunch of little swans swimming near the edge of the water. There were three baby swans. They weren't white like their parents, but fuzzy and grey. They looked so cute. I asked why the babies were a different color? Grammy said the babies are grey when they are born, and will turn white when they grow up.

I asked Grammy if we can get closer to the swans to get a better look.

So we went off the bridge and walked towards the baby swans. I was so excited to see them and started walking faster!

As we got closer the mama swan came out of the water squawking and flapping her feathers. She started making so much noise and running towards us. Grammy yelled "Quick, we need to get out of here! Let's run!" We ran back to the bridge.

I never saw Grammy move that fast before!

Finally, the mama swan went back to her babies. "What happened? Why did she chase us?" I asked.

Grammy explained that the big swan was the mother of the baby swans. She thought we might hurt her babies, and she was protecting them. Animals usually don't come near people that way, unless they feel someone might hurt them. The Mama swan was scared we were getting too close to her family. She was just protecting her children.

It's important to respect animals from a distance. They don't know if we will hurt them. There are some people who might do that.

After we rested on the bridge, Grammy said she had enough excitement for today and we headed home. We can go on another hike tomorrow if I want to. I answered "Yes, I do! I really had fun today!"

The next day after breakfast, Grammy said since I did so well yesterday, we will climb a mountain today! Not a really big one, but one that will be perfect for us!

Grammy packed us lunch. We brought sandwiches, apples, and some water. Then we were off to find another adventure!

When we arrived in the woods, there were different trails we could take. Each trail had a colored flag. There was a red one, blue one or a yellow one. Grammy told me that if you get lost, you can follow the color markings to help guide you through the woods.

As soon as we went into the woods. It started to get dark. I asked Grammy "If we are still outside, why did it get darker? Where did the sun go?"

Grammy pointed up. When I looked up, I saw that the trees were so high, with so many big branches. The leaves on the trees blocked the sunlight, and it became darker.

Then we started up the mountain on our journey. I picked the blue trail.

Grammy said let's see how many animals you can find, but don't count the bugs because in the woods there are way too many bugs here! I bet I find more animals than Grammy.

The squirrels were everywhere! I saw a rabbit and some chipmunks. At first, I thought the chipmunks were baby squirrels. Then we saw a lot of birds flying around.

Grammy said I should stop and to stand still and listen. She asked what I heard. I didn't hear anything, but some rustling of tree leaves. She told me to close my eyes, be very still and try to listen again.

This time I heard crickets and birds. Different sounds of all the birds talking to one another. I heard the wind between the trees. "Wow Grammy, I didn't know there were sounds in the woods." It was fun to listen to the different sounds!

When we got to top of the mountain there was a clearing. There were no trees, just a big open area, with tree logs made into benches. So we stopped to look at the beautiful view. You could see houses in the distance and some big buildings. It felt like we were near the clouds. We were at the top of the mountain!

Grammy said this was a good time to take a break and eat our lunch. So we sat on the logs and enjoyed the fresh air and our beautiful view.

We were just about done when we saw a group of deer.

The deer looked like a family with two babies.

Grammy reminded me, "Remember yesterday when we tried to get close to the baby swans? Today, we will just stay still and watch them from a distance." They were still too, and watched us back.

We just were looking at each other, with no one moving! It seemed like a long time!

Grammy got excited and said she had an idea! "Let's leave them our apples." Deer like to eat fruit, they usually eat them right off the trees. We left my apple and Grammys half eaten apple on the tree log and slowly moved away starting back down the mountain. As we slowly left, I kept looking back, and then we saw the whole family eating the apples! They all were sharing and taking bites. It was really cool.

I didn't know I'd like hiking and nature.

I enjoyed hiking with Grammy that summer. I learned a lot about nature and animals. Animals are a lot like people. They have family, love and they protect each other from danger.

Grammy is so smart, she teaches me so many new things, I can't wait till next summer to have another special adventure with my Grammy!

CPSIA information can be obtained
at www.ICGtesting.com
Printed in the USA
BVHW020339140921
616276BV00001B/2